Jupiter's perigee

Jupiter's Perigee

Sophia Hardy

The following poems were first published in the journals attributed below (as Sophia Johnson); many thanks to Poetry NZ and Landfall for their outstanding support of New Zealand poetry.

Driftwood, Poetry NZ Yearbook 2, 2015, *Somewhere in the City*, Poetry NZ no. 49. 2014, *Blake's Angel*, Poetry NZ no. 47. 2013 and *Jupiter is Close*, Landfall no244, 2012

Published by 99% Press,
an imprint of Lasavia Publishing Ltd.
Auckland, New Zealand

www.lasaviapublishing.com

Copyright © Sophia Hardy, 2017
Cover design © Jennifer Rackham, 2017

This book is copyright. Apart from any fair dealing for the purpose of private study, research, criticism or reviews, as permitted under the Copyright Act, no part may be reproduced by any process without the permission of the publishers.

ISBN: 978-0-473-40602-8

For Craig

The road of excess leads to the palace of wisdom.

William Blake

Outline

11 *Jupiter is close*

13 Constance

21 William Blake

27 Jupiter's voyage

31 Will

37 Dadhija

43 William and Lucy

57 The girl

65 The author

Jupiter is close

Perhaps this book will enrich my heart

Perhaps this book
will my voice
effortlessly
speak -
The words
like honey
tumbling into a pitcher of milk
and cinnamon for breakfast

The book
I have it here   under
this old yellow cloth lampshade
on thin mahogany base -
Will it gift the words
       when I talk to you tonight
       over the lagoon
       over mangrove water
to single out the stars
and tell you
that Jupiter is close
and why I clutch your hand

Constance

Constance sees Jupiter

Constance pulled the gliding windows shut
the glass rattled
and the paint job
was not so good
as it could have been

Constance pressed a gold bracelet
on her thin wrist
till it dug her pale green veins
and saw a brighter star
than the others
pulling the black pupils
of her eyes into orbit

'I ought not to drive tonight'
she thought
'I don't want to fall in love'

Constance's flowers

Constance's scentless flowers
were lovely
they glowed brilliant white
in her dark room

And rose before her
in her dreams
squidgy curled petals
of the large barely opened roses
their cut stems

Love, Constance concluded
was for other people

Constance was cold

Constance was too cold for God
she drew her fabric shoulders in
and stitched them
with her arms
in
about her chest

Hateful violets in the distant winter sun
didn't develop velvet thoughts in her

The wind sighed and fell
and died because
through her forest of pressing fingers
and the blunt force of cashmere cloth
it could not reach her heart

Cold, Constance watched the street
in a Greg Lauren shawl
and waited for her taxi

Country house

Constance couldn't see out of the house
that night
it was too black
they never should
have come
to the country

Constance didn't know
what moved the grape vines
what chattered their thick brown stems
what tore their sheer green leaves

Mudbrick should be warmer she thought
soft orange mudbrick
like Tuscany

For a moment
the smell of rosemary
touched her mouth

And she considered leaving

Constance in love

Constance was in love
as stars that fell
and lovers that pointed
fell
in love

Like birch trees
pressed against each other
in a young forest

The thin cutlery set was matched with the heavy cutlery set
and the beeswax candles were melting so fast
yellow against brass green candle sticks

Constance's heart had melted and pooled
and spilled on the dining room table
where the entree soup
and stacked hors d'oeuvres
of smashed broad beans
and blue vein cheese,
and dripping pinot noir
blackened salmon
and swarms of honey sweetened ganache
and clotted cream
dessert wine
elder flower
earthquakes of Chanel scent
and the burning poppy flowers
so long stemmed were
to die for
the tablecloth was un deux trois

Constance left

William Blake

Blake's angel

Date: 1782
William Blake
worn and heavy
head bent to see the rich floorboards
carved an angel into his kitchen table

A long walk around the river-bank
showed the river eating the land
and up in the knotted tree
sat many angels

With shining hair
their muscled arms reached to the sky
to touch God

Blake peeled back the wood
to sculpt their legs
and large foreign feet
swinging in the air

The rain smashed at the roof
always trying to get in
to wet the hewn angel
that lived in Blake's table

Blake's fire

William Blake's fire
made hot the skin of his spine
as he wrote
and the flames pulled the water from the logs
till it spat and seethed

Outside
William Blake pressed his thick hands
into the bark
of the log cabin
his knuckles framed the scorching sky
and the sounds built
from the east
shrieked
like hunting birds

He thought he could feel
the shrieking angel voice
caress the burn marks on his spine

He wrote,
'the celestial voices are much clearer here'

Blake's Jupiter

When the portrait of Jupiter was wrought
only the storm clouds at the window provided muse

*It was outside
on a little wooden table
rain darkened
weed ridden
with feathery moss
to touch beneath her fingertips*

That deep grey day in Albion
the sky was secretly aflame
and the god scorched and drenched
holding power in his creased palms

*It was beneath the table
where the picked clovers wilted
and the sun drained into the shade*

Jupiter was hot with rage
William could hardly contain the raging image
as his heated metal hands would not be engraved

*Beneath the table in the shade
where willow had fallen
delicate green
was a page signed with an X*

Blake's room

Blake had another room
not the one of wood
where the watermarked beams
dripped
with the incessant crying
of the storm

One of stone
with meadow grass on the floor
and dusky gold images of
of the divine

Two figures
disclosed their form
ochre Aphrodite gazing on

A myrtle tree
pressed its grey trunk
and grew up the wall
with a shock of blush coloured flowers

Blake held a tawny haired woman that night
Who was as warm as rain

Night

12 of August 1827
Here lies William Blake

Jupiter's voyage

Jupiter: Sydney to Auckland 1841

There weren't a lot of us on the Jupiter barge
passengers under the lights
pushing off from the soft Sydney shores
like one uses a stick to press away from the edge

There was all this sea
this was our passage

The sky followed its own river
upside down Orion
and his belt of jewels
stolen
and some were missing

Jupiter was nowhere that I could see
we drifted on its namesake

Depths fell beneath us
and it felt colder
as we hit New Zealand
struck its sand

Captain Hicks
was gleaming eyed, salt proud
dark hair wired
stocky shouldered sure
though I lost a shoe to the pulling tide

Will

Dark morning

The spring storms ruffled
his soft hair

A blonde girl smoothed it
by the fire in the bush
as he lay down
turning the stars into birds

One star fell that night
he looked for it
in the dark morning
sure it was somewhere in the roses
the dark, strangely warm roses
whose thorns tore his linen trousers

He did find the star
not many people know

Found

Most of these were lost in the fire

There was a rifle of papers
and gun holes in the tin
trees cracked from the summer storm
and the ever-gentle moss

Things are still charred
the driftwood table for instance will never
a Dr Seuss tree was hurt
the evening air brushed against all things singed
the cast iron tea pot contained a wet meadow and thus was immune

But the poems were lost

Will and Jupiter

He was a hot god
that crept from the campfire
and boiled the blood of the kikuyu grass
savaging its fat yellow stems

It had been all negligence
and wind moving through the dark forest

One of the best things about the darkness
was all the light
the oil lamp in iron and orange windows
of carved wood
the fat drippy candle, probably not beeswax
and all the romanticism left on the table
in a heap
and the stars scrabbling amongst the nikau and the river
overwhelming

When finally Will reached the clearing
out in the open
he had no idea which planet was which

She'd told him about Jupiter
she seemed to know a lot
of where it hung in between
in space

Dadhija

Gold Buddha

Siddhartha could see poverty
draped on her shoulders
and the warm mist
from the dark well
and the dazzling morning moon

His tiny clawed hand dug into her sides

He loved her actuality
the joy with which she walked
towards the dawn

She knelt
on the russet mesh scarf
dust blew through its thin stitches

Each day she asked the sky
for the same
for rain
to drench
to weep down Buddha's gold cheeks
and almond pitted eyes

I'd help, thought Buddha
but I am only a statue

Siddhartha and Jupiter

It was as cold as brass
that had moon
and leaves to fill its metal face

It was as brilliant as the sky
and as warm as the beginning

And little gold Buddha was the middle of the shining garden
his eyes saw shapes and dewy softness
and his rivets ached
the tide had swept all the stars to the northern sky
where they huddled in the long limbed, green tree,
thick with seeds pods

But this was to say nothing
these were merely his percepts of a vast garden with a swing and
Dadhija nearby

His thoughts were all Jupiter
the planet hulking in the centre sky
gazing directly at his thin metal face
in the midst of a summer night

Monsoon

Dadhija spent a lot of time
alone with her soul
she and him in the dark

She asked if he could remember touching her on the cheek
her cheek was soft
but he denied it

There was a water-welt in the bookshelf's varnish
'Remember this?' he asked

She could not remember
the monsoon that rolled down the streets
that trickled down the walls
ruining her grandmother's painting
of the winter tree clutching its soft orange autumn leaf

A hundred faces turned to the rain
and grinned without force
for the desert grew that day
with flushes of silken grass
and trickling streams

'It's a pity that I cannot remember'

Her soul and she lay down
and he pressed his lips to her forehead
to kiss the soft skin there

'But I do remember after the rains
the woman in her garden
burning with moon
under the strong armed tree
talking of love'

William and Lucy

The Harpist (a prelude)

Luckily, the woman you jilted
was deft with her fingers
and wrote down the whole affair
in music for the harp

That's how I knew your name
recognised it on the gravestone
by the willow tree

With rosemary crushed under your fingers
you studied the lines of the dark body
biding by the night-drunk lake

Rare
at depicting bitter ruin
was this young harpist

William and Lucy

The lanterns
wired around trees
make night less dangerous

Illuminated ceiling
of Oaks' locked hands
bobs in the menace-less breeze

William introduces sex
a lantern falls

The grass turns gold then black
from scented dark
- a girl giggles
a thorny branch hits Lucy on the head
she shrieks

Midnight wind
wanting the lantern's fire,
pushes hard on the trees' backs
they moan

Desperately William tramples the spreading fire
whose gold desired the darkness

William starts to notice

William hadn't noticed
that Jupiter was close
he didn't much like science

He had noticed that all the fat
white flowers had fallen on the ground
and the sun was hot
even at night

He had noticed
that Lucy hadn't called
or texted

But he was busy
as the endless sky was busy

Besides, Lucy would like
the necklace he got her
a silver L
on a silver chain

William shows Lucy the sky

They were there
threaded into the clay
William's torch showed their dewy webs
William's feet were close to Lucy's
as he showed her the glow worms

The trees towered
Lucy kept drawing breath in
and in
watching the tiny, shuddering moth
fly toward the lights

Lucy turned for home
William touched her neck

She watched the moth pressing
into the glow worm's shaggy silk
watched it struggle
and stick

William whispered in Lucy's ear
that she should stay and watch the sky move

The moth stopped moving

William lies to Lucy

Lucy touches
her blue cloth box of jewels

She draws a silver chain
with an L on it to wear tonight

There's no knock on the door

Lucy decides on sensible shoes
she can see the street dragging cars towards the coast
can't see William in his blue Mazda
her phone hasn't lit up for an hour

Lucy twists her head
to see Orion's studded belt
looming in the sky

Lucy's phone stays still on her dresser
she takes off her shoes
sits on the bed
and watches Orion walking away to the edge of the sky

Lucy and Zach

Zach watches Lucy
walking past the narrow shops

They lean heavily on the road
where Lucy prances and strides

Zach has Lucy's wallet in his denim back pocket
now she returns to him

Inside the bar
friends merge and press their heads together, grinning

Lucy is shy
she presses her hands into his
the cars stop
and the lamp-posts bend their heads like poppies
frightened of the night sky
and Jupiter

She treads on his foot

Inside the friends revel

Outside on the falling pavement
Zach brings his head close to Lucy's
'come to mine – for a drink'

Lucy and the moon

Lucy's heart is rattled
it shakes in her thin diaphragm cage
the moon large and yellow
has fallen through the flimsy sky
and presses its face up against the city endearingly
begging for attention
it follows the uncertain Lucy
as she drives past summer trees

Lucy didn't care much for the sky
or the fat moon pressing at the window
eagerly showing her the mangrove forest
in the city's shallow sea

Her 'L' chain wrapped around her wrist
her knuckles are scraped
and she smells salt and apple juice

Finally the moon succeeds in sitting next to Lucy
slunk on the passenger seat while she sits at the lights

Joyfully, it starts running its hands over Lucy's face
brilliant with the light of its success
it snuggles into her white cloth shoulder

Finally, she looks at the dark shining city sea
sees sails lit pale yellow and the business towers flashing gold teeth
'All my work' shoots the moon

William and the moon

Of the full moon
William didn't know
for he slept each night that week

A girl told him
through soda teeth
that it was heavy
'pregnant with a mist baby'
and likely to fall

He believed her —
dark flicking eyes
and bottle-clutching hand,
which she dropped
to point at the sky
'It was there'

The blue horizon
said nothing
of the night before

She kicked at the jagged grey gravel
and stared at the paler roofed houses
that met the sky

'I think it fell there'
She pointed limply
with her chubby olive hands
to the south

William goes to Lucy

William loves the roof-tops
the sun gleaming off pale tin
the black cement

William has a secret cigarette
he breathes in its secret smoke
and breathes out a secret breath

The grey fleecy-eared dog
looks defensively at William

The fast cars
were between him and Lucy
and the vanishing brick driveway
and the rosewood door
and the steep stylish stairs of slab wood
and a bedroom hung with the face of a loving moon

William's jealousy

William didn't like the moon much
it was, by association, a bit hippy-dippy
plus he was jealous
of Lucy's newfound affection
for the sky

She told him last night
grateful for the thick stemmed birthday flowers
that Jupiter was close
the closest it has ever been to earth
in living memory

And that the black water
concealed a thousand stars
that would glow if they shook their hands
in the ocean
that the boats in the harbour were nothing to her

The girl

Somewhere in the city

In the breathy
cold darkest blue
a girl dropped a thin yellow shell
threaded on a waxed green string
somewhere in the city

The girl didn't know
- which concrete ripping birch root,
- which metal arched bridge,
- which cold turfed jolting pier,
- which headland of shaking lights,
had grabbed it

The girl realised the sky was falling
thick and fast
pieces of midnight hit her
and the cerulean stars threatened

The girl's barren neck
bent to search the iron gutter grate
for her necklace
her thin yellow shell necklace
that still smelt of fresh cut grass

Jupiter and the girl

The girl saw Jupiter
sparkling near the moon

'Perhaps,
it is a space station'
she thought

'For there are never bright stars
over the city at 10'

The girl wore gloves
for it was cold that night

And her soft black gloves
hugged herself
as she stood under 20
interlocking trees

Pressed her forehead into her arm
so her hot eyes
could look away
from Jupiter

Time and the girl

Time sits waiting in an alley, bored, wondering why the girl in the red scarf
has passed him so many times, curling her hair around her fingers
vivaciously. What did she want? He pulls himself up
against the wall, breathing into his collar.
He has some idea what. His legs are lazy
and the clock tower seems to pull
on his heavy arms with each tick.
Again she passes, head down,
this time wishful, she turns
and looks up, catching
his snarling eyes and
in the deep hazel,
he figures that
he loves
her.

That
he loves
her, he figures
and in the deep hazel
catching his snarling eyes
she turns and looks up, wishful,
this time head down, again she passes.
With each tick seems to pull on his heavy
arms and the clock tower. His legs are lazy. He
has some idea what, breathing into his collar he pulls
himself up against the wall. What did she want? curling
her hair around her fingers vivaciously, has passed him so many times.

Jupiter finds the girl

Jupiter caught up with the girl in a dark way that only god's know
a shadow on the street
as hot as metal
the girl had never been to the stars
so she did not know
the feeling that gripped the street
with tar

She did not understand
the depth of her misery
till the god held her jaw
and pulled her into the inside of the inside
surprisingly there were trees there
a dark landscape and hillside
not leading to the sea
but curling around a wine dark pool
always dark like rich red wine
there was no moon there for there needn't be

And she was far gone
in Jupiter's embrace
anyway
she had left alone, alone
and now forgot herself

And in his perfect fingers
Jupiter held up her lost necklace
given to her on a sweet night
before Christmas day

Angels on Franklin Road

The flock of leaves surrendered
to the moon
which forced its way
down to the street

The tapestry of houses yielded
to the lamps
which escaped with the moon
to the street

And there the vandalized dalliance
of rock and water, and mouth
made the angels gasp in the mingled light

Aphrodite stood draped in Zambesi black
with a hood and a mask and an olive branch
the mask was all feathers
the hood was silk and the olive branch was dead

But the sidewalk was a coast of cheerful violets
where the oblivious lovers lay

The author

The hidden blues of the sky

God came out of the clouds in the evening
I'd waited for him all day
staring at the blinding sun

Then on the darkening salty rock
with my toes pressed into the barnacled edge
I saw the sky open every white of the sun
saw the sea bright and the hidden blues of the sky

And in the gentle blinding evening night
I clasped my soul with sandy hands
and walked home through the night to my lover

Wednesday is tomorrow

To Marry, Wednesday is tomorrow!
and Monday is today
I lost a day to one of Jupiter's moons
I lost a year
the earth forgot to orbit the sun
and nothing could contain my shock
when the spring daffodils pressed their closed swan heads out of the ground

No, I did not see this coming
but I said yes
and you knelt down
the kitchen was a mess

But now tomorrow is Wednesday
and I will marry you

In Jupiter's orbit

Somewhere in the silent naivety of Christmas
our arms outstretched holding candles in the dark
and their yellow flames
inferior to the
distant fire of Jupiter
thundering close now
the waves smashed on the hardened sand

Our pale secret forearms
made unknown
supplication
to the heaven
of black water
reflecting the riot of the burning planet
in a hot damp sky

We fell from Time
like the dark sliding of water over rock

It seemed 100 sleek canoes rode towards us
and William Blake pointed at a falling star

Driftwood

None of my friends have grown up
some of them died on the beach
rushing under the phosphorus waves
to join the stars underwater

And those that remain
play Pick Up Sticks
with the skinny white driftwood

They buried their wedding rings
in the sand that night
with the embers
so that the beach did not go up in flames

Venus on the way down

The earth was turned upside down late last night
the stars fell on the damp grass
thick redwoods crashed into each other
and made a mess of pine and sap

That pink satin dress I had was dipped in mud
with threads exposed

You seemed unshaken
arms still lover's branches
not worried about the flood of broken leaves and the raw sky
hissing as the sea hit its fires

It was almost as if the sawdust and clay didn't slip beneath your feet
as if your head didn't race towards the treetops
catching a glimpse of Venus on your way down

Little gold book

It's here
By the statue of the gold girl
or is she yellow
her hair is wheat

Mind the stolen shells
we took them from Spirit's Bay
under a blood moon
I remember the wooden hotel
and the isolation

I dreamed of the highwayman that night
riding under a broken sky
on the dusk blue road
a mask dripping from his face

I woke to see
- dark wine in glasses
- ten people still talking at midnight
- my face softened with salt tears

Here it is
the little gold book
perhaps this book will enrich my heart

www.ingramcontent.com/pod-product-compliance
Lightning Source LLC
Chambersburg PA
CBHW021413290426
44108CB00010B/506